Public Speaking Without Fear

How to overcome your anxiety and present with confidence

By

Clare Cairns

First Published in Great Britain by Class Moustache Books.

This paperback edition published in 2019 by Class Moustache Books www.class-moustache.com

www.professionalperformanceassociation.com

A CIP catalogue record for this book is available from the British Library ISBN: 978-1-9995833- 4-7 - Public Speaking Without Fear: How to overcome your anxiety and present with confidence (paperback)

10 9 8 7 6 5 4 3 2 1

Book by Clare Cairns

Cover Illustration © 2019 by Clare Cairns and Business Logo Designs

"For my daughter (who was only a few weeks old when this book was published). May you always speak your truth and empower those who cannot."

Contents

Chapter One: Why Acting? 1

Chapter Two: The Pressure System 5

Chapter Three: Preparation 9

Chapter Four: Rehearsal..17

Chapter Five: Emotions 27

Chapter Six: Super Objective...41

Chapter Seven: Stress 45

Chapter Eight: Uniform...51

Chapter Nine: Role-Play 55

Chapter Ten: Energy...63

Chapter Eleven: Congratulations!...71

Chapter One
Why Acting?

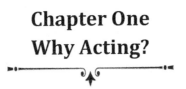

Let me start by saying, I never called myself a public speaking *expert*. It was others who bestowed this title upon me. As soon as they did, I started to feel nervous. In some respects my job just became even harder. Speaking in public about *any* topic can be difficult but speaking about public speaking, as a *public speaking ex- pert*, applies even more pressure. Surely, I should be the best Public Speaker in the world to qualify for this title.

Luckily I soon realised my job was not to be the best public speaker in the world; it was to train people to become the best. And when I say the best, I mean the best for them. Not everyone needs to be a high-powered influential leader. Some people just want to get out there and enjoy it rather than pull a sick day at work or pretend a distant relative has died, just to get out of speaking in public.

Yes, I've heard all the excuses and felt all the pain.

I started life as an actor and singer. In 2004, I set up my own drama school in Scotland called Acting Out, where I have trained thousands of performers at all levels in acting, singing, directing and public speaking. I worked in Europe, America and Australia with a variety of high profile actors, writers, directors and speakers as well as huge organisations and World Class Universities. In

2017, I set up another company dedicated to corporate speaking training, and in 2019 I established The Professional Performance Association (and The PPA Club), which offers an exclusive online membership for public speaking training. My main training tool for all clients, corporate industries, online members and private educational institutions was and still is derived from the principles of Acting and Performing.

Why Acting and Performing?

Let me ask you something. It's the same question I ask all my clients during their first session with me.

Do you know a professional actor who has trouble speaking in public?

I'm pretty sure you just said "No".

And I agree. So far, 100% of the professional actors I know are absolutely fine when speaking in public (and I know quite a few). This is because they have been trained in the majority of skills that any good speaker needs, such as a strong voice, controlled energy, relaxed body, good breath work, stage presence and a huge knowledge of role-play and acting itself. Yes, some actors get nervous, but the difference between them and the normal public speaker is that nerves don't affect the actor's performance or presentation.

Unfortunately, we don't get taught these essential skills at school (at least not in the UK). Performing Arts is pretty low on the curriculum priority, even though virtually every professional role now involves some form of public speaking and presenting.

In fact, your boss probably expects you to stand up in front of a hundred people and give your monthly report without so much as a thought. Maybe they want you to lead a team meeting or deliver workshops to other staff, even though they have never supplied you with any form of training to help you do this. For most employment nowadays, you are simply expected to become this amazing speaker, even though you have no experience, no skills and probably no idea where to start. I bet some of you who are reading this don't even know how to warm up your voice properly, despite the fact you use your voice as one of your main tools at work (assuming you speak to people on the phone or face-to-face on a daily basis).

There are so many people losing sleep, feeling stressed and dreading public speaking events simply because - right now - they lack the knowledge and the training to let themselves succeed.

And that's why I created "The Pressure System", wrote this book and created the online program.

I have been coaching people in public speaking for many years. In the last eight years, I have been using the same system time and time again with 100% success. For some people the success is life changing, for others it's an improvement. Absolutely everyone I've coached using The Pressure System methods has gained something valuable, even if that's just a good night's sleep before their presentation the following day. And for anyone who suffers from anxiety, you'll know how important that is.

For me, this means the system works. It's effective, it's useful, and it's a positive tool that everyone should try. The Pressure System's original foundation comes from acting and performing, but it's been moulded and developed into presenting and speaking. It also goes beyond this. Many of the steps you learn here, you can apply to everyday life. In fact, I encourage you to do this! The more practice you gain, the quicker you will become at using these skills when you really need them (like speaking in public).

Chapter Two
The Pressure System

So why is it called "The Pressure System"?

Like the weather, public speaking can be extreme. You can go through spells when it's okay, then all of a sudden it becomes dark. Full of thick grey clouds that you can't see past. You have no idea why or how it changed so quickly or came on so strong. The grey clouds close in to become a dense fog which gets thicker and thicker, heavier and heavier, until the fog completely consumes you. You can't see through it. You can't get out of it. You can't speak or move. All hopes of a perfect, easy, relaxed presentation have gone. You can't speak or think. You have a total blank.

This is what I call: Public Speaking Crisis.

Public Speaking Crisis can happen at any time. You might be a very accomplished speaker who still experiences lots of pressure, nerves and worry. You might have changed roles, left university or embarked on a new business venture. The point is, it doesn't matter who you are or where you have come from, sometimes you can't predict how you will feel on a given day or how a presentation will go.

So it's better to be prepared. Have your waterproofs in your bag in case it gets wet. Or a hat in case the sun gets too hot.

That's what the Pressure System gives you. *The tools to be prepared.* And it offers this to you in the shortest amount of time possible. You'll notice I don't pad out chapters to make the book bigger. It's designed specifically to change your patterns of thinking and the way you approach your public speaking events, *fast.* For some people, this really does happen overnight. For others it may take a bit longer.

The Pressure System is also easy to remember. The word "PRESSURE" contains the initial letters of the key components you need to ensure a successful event.

These are: Preparation, Rehearsal, Emotions, Super Objective, Stress, Uniform, Role-Play and Energy. What's great is that you can focus on any of these at any time. You don't need to go through them in a chronological sequence, although for ease of ticking off your public speaking checklist, it works chronologically too.

A Few Fundamentals...

The most important advice I can give you before you begin is to trust yourself and trust this method. Complete all the practice exercises. I know it's tempting to skim over them, but they are there for a good reason. If you have an open mind, a desire to improve and a willingness to change, then you will succeed.

There are a couple of other things to mention too. Firstly, *you are not alone.* It may feel like you are the only person in your team, your profession or your group of friends or family who is going through public speaking crisis. But you are not.

Rest assured, it's perfectly normal to feel nervous and even anxious when presenting, speaking in public or attending an interview. Luckily for us, some of the biggest and most talented stars in Hollywood had a fear of public speaking, including Julia Roberts, Samuel L Jackson and Bruce Willis, so they took up drama and got into acting. And some of them still avoid the limelight today! So the good news is:

You are normal.

I'm also going to tell you something that you don't want to hear. You are not special.

And I mean that in the best possible way.

As far as public speaking goes, your stress is not unique. In fact, speaking in public is one of our biggest worries and most common fears, according to Dwyer & Davidson (2012) and Richmond, Wrench, & McCroskey (2013). In some cases, survey responses have suggested public speaking to be a bigger fear than death! So I will pose this simple question: Would you rather die or deliver a presentation?

I'm 99.9% sure that you chose the latter.

When speaking in public, *you should be nervous.* I get nervous.

But reading this book and learning about the Pressure System is going to provide you with all the tips, tricks and tools you need to survive and to succeed every time you present, talk or perform in public.

And please give yourself some credit here. You are taking time out of your busy life to improve yourself.

This is a very positive start to your transformation into a public speaking pro!

Chapter Three

Preparation

Preparation plays a big part in how well your presentation, speech or interview goes. In my experience, there is a direct link between nerves and lack of preparation. The more prepared you are, the less strain you put on yourself and consequently the less anxious you feel.

Let's assume you are the sort of person who is very likely to prepare. Buying and reading a book takes a bit of effort, as does researching which book to buy. The word "research" is very important here. It applies to whatever subject you are preparing to discuss.

In other words, **know your topic.** Understand what you are speaking about inside out. You are then less likely to be "caught off guard" and feel like an impostor during your speech. In turn, this will reduce your nervousness.

If you are the sort of person who tries to "wing it" then I suggest you stop leaving it to chance, do the ground work and give yourself a real shot at being a good public speaker.

To script or not to script: That is the question.

In the first step of the Pressure System, I usually get asked: should I use a script? *A script is when the speaker writes out word for word what they are going to say.*

In acting, unless we are using improvisation or devising techniques, an actor always has a script. You may be surprised to learn then, that my advice to 99% of my clients is AVOID SCRIPTS in public speaking. And here are a few reasons why.

When someone asks you to deliver a speech or a presentation, they want you to talk to them. Not read to them. Otherwise they would say "Could you do a *reading* at the next seminar?" Or better still, they would simply ask you to email the document to all the attendees of the event to save people from leaving their desks. Public speaking is about *Speaking*. Not Reading. You want to talk to people, engage with them and let them feel part of your presentation.

When you have a script, your energy and voice tend to go down towards that script. You look up for the sake of creating the illusion of eye contact, not because you are speaking to people but because you were told to look up every three seconds by your school teacher when you were 7 years old.

Unless you are an amazing story-teller and can speak words from a page as though they were not written at all, your presentation is already far less interesting for the listener. In fact this is exactly what *they* become, a listener. Not an audience. As a performer (which you *are* when you speak in public), you want an audience. A live interaction of energies that can give you a boost when you see people are interested. Maybe they laugh at your joke or cry when you need to hit home on a sad reality. Unless you are at a professional actor's standard, reading rarely induces the same genuine reaction.

Having a script also means there is no room for any deviation, even when your circumstance demands one, such as having a lively audience and wishing you could interact more. Or the opposite may occur, when your audience is not responsive and it's very difficult to improvise if the script isn't working.

You could lose your place at any moment and experience that gaping silence while you try to find your place again.

Overall, having a script and preparing to use it, means you have to stick with it, come what may.

There are so many words in a script and usually lots of pages to get through. When you are reading, there is a tendency to *get to the end*. To finish it. Imagine you are fluttering through the pages while all those faces are looking at you. Your nerves will likely be on a higher scale than normal. Your heart rate increases, your speech quickens and even though you took your time when you practised it at home, suddenly you feel under pressure to rush through your presentation.

We can attribute this to three common factors.

1. You want to get this over with as quickly as possible be-cause you hate speaking in public

2. You are not seeing a response from your audience and you fear that you are boring them or that they think you don't deserve to be there

3. You are nervous and have limited control over your tempo, voice or brain functions

Although the last point can still happen without a script, in my experience, it's much more likely to happen *with* a script.

Even with this knowledge, I can understand the thoughts and fears that may be going through your head right now.

What if I forget what I am talking about?

What if all those faces put me off?

I've heard many reasons for not binning-the-script in my time and I assure you, while you may think your script is your "safety net"... it's still *a net.* It restricts you, entangles you and makes it almost impossible for you to be a free-flowing public speaker.

So, what's the best way to prepare to ensure you will remember what to say?

In my opinion, the best way to prepare for your presentation or speaking event is to gather together all your relevant facts and exactly what you would like to cover. Then use bullet points on cue cards.

For example, let's say you want to talk about your experience with public speaking and how you got over your fear.

You may start by recalling your worst experience, then follow on with what you did training wise (maybe you read this book, enrolled onto a course, etc). Then you discuss how you eventually overcame your fear, before you summarise, leaving your audience with something memorable to think about.

I would recommend you use three small index cards. These are great because if you are nervous they won't shake like A4 paper. On each card, write a heading and up to three bullet points.

For example:

Bad Experience

- Big work conference, trying to impress boss

- Used a script, kept stumbling over lines, no-one laughed at jokes

- Felt embarrassed

Training

- Researched who could help me

- Read this book

- Gained the skills I needed and realised I could do this

Good Result

- Next event I had more confidence, no script

- Looked at audience, interacted more, stayed calm

- Brilliant feedback, boss impressed

During your rehearsal, it's likely that as you start to build the structure of your speech, certain words will come to mean more to you and they will *trigger* the response automatically. For example, in the cards above, after just 3 weeks of preparation and rehearsal, the title "GOOD RESULT" may be all you need to start talking about the success of the next event, where you had more confidence, no script, received great feedback and impressed your boss. Therefore "GOOD RESULT" becomes your cue word or trigger response, meaning you won't need the rest of your notes on the day.

You may also find you have more cards/notes than you really need, especially in the initial stages of your preparation. It's important that you resist the temptation to expand every bullet point with a paragraph of information. Keep it short and to the point. Be ruthless. Do you really need a card entitled "INTRODUCTION" with a bullet point saying "My name is...." or "My job is..."?

You are not likely to forget your own name or simple things about yourself or a topic you know very well.

If you overload the cards with unnecessary information and even sentences, it will likely hinder your presentation because it becomes more like a script again.

The beginning of your presentation is a great place to make sure you are engaging with the audience. It's the part where most of what you say you will know very well and don't need to mention in your cards. Such as "My name is" or "Today I'm going to talk to you about...".

If you write this information down, you will start your speech with a strong focus on your cards and *not* on your audience. If you focus on your audience first (by omitting this obvious information from your cards) you have already built an interaction with them at the very beginning, that makes your talk easier in the long run. This is the same for your conclusion. You want to look at your audience, talk to them, engage with them. After all, they are there for you, not your notes.

Let's talk about YOU!

One of the biggest problems for most people when it comes to presentations, is having to talk about themselves. It's an area in most people's lives that is seriously neglected, despite it being an extremely important and powerful tool for your professional success.

Well, I have some good news! Because you've bought my book, you'll get exclusive access to my special bonus training so you can create and deliver an incredible keynote presentation, about you.

In this secret bonus, I'll take you through my step by step formula which will show you exactly how to find your story (the genuine one that moves people) plus how to create and deliver it in a way that is authentic and meaningful. This will ensure you build a true, ever-lasting connection to your audience.

I even include a template you can use to make it super easy!

Download it for free at:

**https://www.professionalperformanceassocia-
tion.com/Book_Bonus_Training**

TOP TIP

You can't prepare for everything. Someone could have an annoying cough. The fire alarm could go off. Technology may not work. You don't have 100% control over everything on the day. What you can control is how much preparation and effort you put in. Approaching public speaking with a positive and pre- pared state of mind is one of the best ways to ensure success.

Chapter Four
Rehearsal

Let's talk about Brain Freeze.

You know how it starts. Your heart pounds in your chest. Your hands get clammy. Your stomach folds into itself. You start to sweat. Your breaths become shorter. Your voice is weak or trembling. Your mouth is dry. Your knees are shaking. Your face flushes red. Everyone is staring at you. Suddenly you stop thinking about yourself and focus on *them*.

The audience.

They see you are nervous. They know you have forgotten what you were going to say. Maybe they think you can't do your job properly. Maybe you *can't* do your job properly. Maybe you don't deserve to be there... maybe they will know you are false.... Maybe.... maybe....and then...

Brain Freeze.

It's amazing how many people prepare well for a presentation and then still get Brain Freeze when it comes to the delivery.

It's one of the most common problems I see as a public speaking coach. Speakers have researched their topic, put their slides together, gone over the slides a million times in front of the computer, editing as they practise until they are happy. Then they turn up on the day of the event, stick in their USB, look up at the audience and BOOM!

The reality of the situation suddenly hits them. People, faces, eyes. Silence. Waiting for *you* to speak, to lead, to teach or to fail.

I know how horrible this feels and how terrifying it can be. But let's begin by explaining why this happens.

When you prepare your presentation in front of your computer, your brain is *situation learning* your talk.

Situated Learning is a theory developed by Jean Lave and Etienne Wenger in the early 1990s which suggests that learners are more likely to learn by actively participating in the real activities of the learning experience. Learning is therefore relative to the learning environment.

In other words, if you learn your presentation in front of your computer without considering the bigger picture such as the venue, the audience, whether you will be standing in front of a podium or walking around the space, your learning experience will be very limited.

When it comes to presenting your talk in front of your audience, you are attempting to transfer your learned talk to a completely different situation. You are expecting your brain to automatically transfer this talk from the learned experience of sitting in front of a computer by yourself, to standing up and performing in front of a large audience in what might be an auditorium, lecture hall, etc. The two situations are very different. Your brain has learned to produce this talk exactly as you have been practising. In front of your computer, talking to yourself and your screen. Not presenting to many people in a large room.

And so your brain freezes as it attempts to rewire itself under vast amounts of pressure. For some people, the brain does manage this... eventually. That is why the beginning of your talk can often be your lowest point and your most nerve-wracking. If after a few minutes into your talk you seem to "click" into the rhythm of things and you begin to relax, then you will know this is your brain adjusting your talk to the new setting.

Luckily, this type of Brain Freeze is purely down to Rehearsal (or lack thereof) and it's easy to fix.

Rehearsal in not sitting in front of your computer. Rehearsal is practising your piece on your feet, doing exactly what you would do on the day (or as close as you can to replicate the environment and situation). Most of this will be using your imagination. Visualising the room, the projector, the screen, the lectern, the podium, the audience, the faces, the eyes. Practise your speech the way you want to deliver it on the day. Then when you finally get to present, your *body* - and more importantly your *brain* - will be ready.

Think about an actor. He doesn't just learn his lines, turn up on stage and go for it. He spends many days, weeks and months rehearsing the scene, the situation, the character and the pace and tone of delivery. These are all key to his performance. And he can only achieve this through proper rehearsal. Even in the beginning stages, while the actor learns his lines in the privacy of his own home, he is very much aware that he will eventually be performing this on stage or on set, with other actors. *That knowledge is always there for him.*

For public speakers, we almost have a harder job because we rarely get to practice in the space we will perform beforehand. So we've got to start getting our brain and body ready from the outset. After we prepare our presentation, we have to start rehearsing as soon as we can.

The purpose of rehearsal is not just to avoid Brain Freeze. It's a very important part of your preparation stage. In fact, the structure of your piece is likely to change based on what you learn and *feel* during the rehearsal process.

For example, you may find that during your rehearsal you keep stumbling over the same slide (no matter how many times you go over it). Normally this indicates there is an issue with the flow of your piece, which is usually down to problems with the structure. *Realising* this stumble is a sign that something isn't right. And it allows you to recognise the issue, investigate and change it. If you hadn't rehearsed, you may have missed the issue and got tongue-tied during your delivery on the actual day of the event.

Therefore, rehearsal also improves the structure of your presentation as well as your delivery of it.

It's important to mention that the flow of your talk will also change as you begin to *improvise* around the topics (rather than reading them directly from a script). Each time you rehearse you will be saying the same thing slightly differently, which builds more connections in your brain thus enhancing your brain's ability to retrieve stored information on the day.

As you may already know, the brain is made up of billions of neurons which are nerve cells that communicate with each other by sending chemical messages and signals. As you learn something new, such as your presentation topic, your neurons send and receive information about the presentation. As you practise, or in our case rehearse, your neural pathways become more and more efficient as they wire together and connections between them strengthen. Consequently, they take less time to signal to each other and communicate.

While you rehearse, you are building and strengthening the neurological pathways more and more around your topic, giving you better, easier and quicker access to your knowledge base. You will not only become better at speaking about your topic and presentation, but you will also become quicker when *thinking* about it too.

This improves both your understanding of your talk, your delivery and your confidence. You'll be acquiring knowledge faster and with much more ease every time you rehearse.

Rehearsal also helps you with the Question and Answer session at the end of your presentation. Being put on the spot and unable to prepare for every question asked can be a very stressful part of any presentation. Yet, if you have rehearsed and effortlessly wired all these neuron connections, you and your brain will be very familiar with speaking about the topic in many different ways and retrieving the information you need using *different* brain connections and neurological pathways. When using a script, you don't get this *extra training* as you are only going over your topic one way.

And the extra benefits of rehearsal don't stop there.

As you rehearse your presentation and speak about your topic in many different ways, you are also building your improvisational skills, an actor's most useful tool.

Improvisation is what we do when we create something spontaneously, normally with very little preparation. It's a skill actors and public speakers need as they are constantly put on the spot, having to come up with ideas, answers or explanations that they haven't necessarily prepared for. By developing improvisation skills, speakers become more confident in their ability to "trust elves" and "just go for it".

There are many times in life and business when you are called to do just that. And it's not always easy! For example, during work meetings when you need to get your point across and deliver your opinion or report with clarity and confidence. When the stakes are high, it's essential your team and audience trust you. And improvisation-confidence will really help!

Luckily, there are lots of easy exercises you can do to improve your improvisation skills. I have a whole module on this in my online program, Public Speaking Without Fear, as well as easy exercises to improve how you speak on the spot.

If you find "speaking up" hard or feel it's an area you need to improve, check out my program at:

www.professionalperformanceassociation.com

Because you are reading my book, I'm going to give you a special coupon code too. Use READBOOK at checkout to save money and get the program for super cheap.

In the mean time, my favourite exercise involves choosing a topic - any topic - and speaking about it for 30 seconds on the spot, with no preparation or preplanning. Just keep speaking until your 30 seconds is up!

Another common issue I am asked to address, particularly for clients overseas, is how to remember what to say when you are speaking in a language that is not your native tongue.

Well, the above explanation about your brain connections holds true for a second language - your brain connects to different pathways and different ways of expressing what you mean. For example, you may cover the same meaning using a slightly different vocabulary. To reiterate your point (in English) you may say: "Therefore" for the first time, "Consequently" the second time, "Thus" the next time, and on the day of your presentation you might say: "In conclusion". Your knowledge base of word retrieval is strengthened by the continued re-wiring of your brain on this particular topic. This makes any language barriers, or lack of vocabulary variation, less likely to occur and so improves your delivery and confidence.

But let's be honest, even mid-way through your talk, Brain Freeze may still occur. It may be triggered by an external factor like an audience member looking bored, or an internal factor like nerves. However, if you have rehearsed many times then your brain will be *used* to finding the information and speaking about it *on the spot*, because you've already gone over your talk slightly differently 100 times before. You will find it easier to get back on track without losing self-control and without fiddling with papers while your audience cringe in their seats.

Practice makes perfect...

This is a brilliant statement! It's the one your parents or teachers told you when you were "no good" at something and wanted to give up. It taught you to be committed. However, for public speaking, it doesn't necessarily apply. Instead I like to say:

Practice makes perfect, if you are practising in the right way.

You see, practice can make perfect (or close to it) if you are practising **in the way that works best for you.**

Clients who come to me with this "practice makes perfect" phrase are very often people who have little idea of what public speaking actually is. Each time they subject themselves to "more practice" they only experience more public failure. Far from attaining perfection, they repeat the same cycle because they never change their style, approach or knowledge base.

To quote Albert Einstein:

"Insanity is doing the same thing over and over again, but expecting different results."

There is a much higher chance people would improve their public speaking if they enrolled onto a course or trained with an expert (or read this book, as you are right now). Doing all these things means you are starting to change patterns and build your knowledge and skill base, which allows you to reap the rewards of good practice, instead of repeating the same failing cycle.

To highlight another misconception; enrolling onto a course where you *just practise* and get *feedback by other students* is not a course. It can often be a recipe for disaster. Let's look at sport for an example.

Say you want to take up golf. You wouldn't turn up to the golf course and start playing a round, would you? You would most likely enrol onto a beginners class where you are coached some basic techniques by a professional.

For people who want to improve their public speaking, going to classes where you deliver a talk and get feedback from non-experts is basically like turning up to a golf range and having people who are practising in their bays turn around and say, "Maybe if you bent your right knee more," or "try to bring your left hand round more like this...."

A professional golfer's coaching nightmare!

The truth is, everyone suddenly becomes an "expert" in public speaking when you ask them to listen to your speech. Family members and fellow public speaking students are not experts. Yes, it's good to practise in front of people, but take everything they say with a pinch of salt. At the end of the day, do comments such as "that was rubbish," or "you're the best speaker in the world," really help? Let me ask you another question. How serious are you about being a good public speaker? Are you willing to invest time and money into your training?

If you are thinking about enrolling onto a course, always check WHO will be giving you feedback and make sure it's the expert tutor of the class, not a joint collaboration with non-experts. And remember, being an "experienced public speaker" doesn't mean the person is an experienced public speaking *coach*.

The good news is that once you and your colleagues have trained in public speaking, your opinions on each other's deliveries will have a great deal of value. The difference is, by then you will have knowledge behind you, something you didn't have before. Your approach to public speaking will have evolved, developed and improved, hence you are no longer "insane" by Einstein's reckoning.

In fact, challenging and developing each other is not only perfectly healthy and good for your skill, it's also a great way to keep learning and improving. There is a lot of research on collaborative learning and how useful it is for academic achievement. That's why I set up the Professional Performance Association (The PPA Club) in the first place. It's somewhere you can share your experiences, up-level and transform your skill and connect with others. You can also ask me questions during live interactive sessions, such as "how much should I rehearse?" or "can I over-rehearse?".

Remember, everyone has their own way to shine in public speaking.

In Acting, no 2 actors play the same role the same way. Brad Pitt doesn't play his roles like Anthony Hopkins would. This is because characters are based on the actor's own experiences, personality and their interpretation of the text using their imagination. The same applies to you as a public speaker.

You might be a natural walker, moving around the space as you talk. Perhaps standing still with your arms by your sides does not work for you. You might need more energy, you might need less energy. You are 100% unique, and the way you speak in public reflects this.

You will get more from presentations, interviews and speeches by letting your natural state, pace and energy flow.

And you will start to realise *what that natural state is* and *what it means to you* through the power of *rehearsal*.

Get up on your feet. Rehearse and see what happens.

TOP TIP

When you are rehearsing, make sure you do it the exact same way you would do it on the day (or as closely as you can). Stand up, walk around. Imagine using powerpoint, looking at the projector screen, then back at the audience. Imagine using the mic, taking questions and answering them. All these little things you do when you practise make it easier for you and your brain on the day.

Chapter Five

Emotions

One of the most important tools for an actor and public speaker is the ability to *be aware of oneself*. That is really what it all comes down to in the Pressure System.

You will have "experts" and well-meaning non-experts tell you what not to do, for example: "stop going red", "stop shaking", "stop stuttering", "stop stumbling", "stop losing your place" or "stop saying Em!"

But this type of feedback and guidance is useless because these issues are common signs of something deeper, more fundamental. We've got to get to the *root* of your problems. And the best way to do that is to know yourself better. Understand your own vulnerability and embrace it.

A helpful technique is to ask yourself why these types of things are happening and then answer in the shortest, most simple and honest way. It's a great start to get you reflecting on *what* is the issue and *why*.

For example, your issue might be that during a presentation, your face goes red and you want to change that.

So ask yourself, "Why am I going red?"

Your answer might be, "Because I'm embarrassed." So ask yourself, "Why am I embarrassed?"

Your answer could be, "Because all these people are staring at me."

Then reflect on this.

Question: "So I'm uncomfortable in this situation?"

Answer: "Yes, I think so."

Question: "What can I do to help this?"

Answer: "Relax and bring my nerves under control so I feel confident."

Don't worry, we cover relaxation and nerves soon. But getting to the core of WHY your body reacts like this really helps.

This is because your body manifests your emotions. So being aware and in control of your emotions is fundamental. These emotions will either work for you, or expose you! Rest assured, most of the negative emotions you feel can be changed if you first recognise them and are aware of why they are occurring.

It's time to start acting.

Let's do a practice exercise!

Walk around your living room, or somewhere with a bit of space. I'm going to suggest some emotions to you and I would like you to feel this emotion in the pit of your stomach (really imagine you feel this way) and walk around the space accordingly. Notice and feel what happens to your body with every emotion.

Walk around the room like you are *excited.*

Find something you are excited about, feel it in your stomach and take off!

What's your body doing? What is your chest doing? How straight is your back? What are your hands doing? How fast or slow are you walking? Be aware.

Now change this emotion to *sad.*

What is your body doing now? How fast or slow are you walking? Is your eye gaze high or low? What is your head doing?

Now change it to *happy.*

It's like excited but more balanced. What are your arms doing? Where are your feet pointing when you walk? How fast are you walking? Are you looking straight ahead or all around or towards the floor? How does it feel?

Now change it to *stressed.*

You've got loads to do and not enough time to do it!

What is your pace like now? What is your jaw doing? Is it tight or locked? What about your eyebrows? Are they raised, or lowered into a frown? Where is your eye gaze? What are you doing with your hands?

Now change it to *confident!*

You are on your way to a public speaking event. You are prepared, you are knowledgeable, you are ready to present and you are feeling good!

What is your posture like? What's your mouth doing? Is your

head high or low? What's your energy like? Have you got lots, or hardly any? How does this feel to you?

Generally, most people will realise that it feels good to have positive emotions. Your body becomes more open, you can breathe more easily and your mind is clearer and more focused. Some people will find positive emotions harder to feel, while for others, it will be the opposite.

But you may have begun to realise how easy it can be to change your emotions after you become aware of them.

Let's look at this in more detail. You probably found you could go from one extreme emotion to the other and still get in touch with the basics of that emotion. For example, from excited to sad. There was likely to be at least *some* change. Therefore, it is very possible to change your emotions if you have awareness of them, and then the intention to change them. *And you are not even an actor!*

Your task now is to become aware of your emotions and how you feel in any given circumstance. Recognise that at particular moments in time you feel "sad" or "nervous" or "anxious". Then think of the emotion that would better serve you at this time. If it is before a presentation, or you just want to feel and appear more positive, try "confident", "excited", or "happy".

Then see what happens.

Let's try another exercise.

This works well if you are in a public place such in the office or in a pub. You can do it in private too and practise the skill.

Be aware of how you feel right now.

Write it down or just think about it.

I want you to change it.

Be confident.

Head up, shoulders back.

Walk or sit with pride and openness!

Now, if you are in a public place, watch what happens around you. Do more people look at you? How are people reacting to you? Any difference? How do you feel inside?

Being confident (or appearing confident) in what you are talking about is one of the key attributes of any good speaker. You don't have to be a confident person, but you should be confident in what you are saying and the particular topic you are speaking about.

Remember, your confidence will be improved by good preparation and lots of rehearsal. Being aware and actively changing your emotions works. Have the desire to feel better! Pull your shoulders back, lift your head up and add a bit more self-assurance to your body!

Practise being aware of your emotions and changing them as often as you can. Make them all positive. As soon as you feel yourself slipping into negative states, try to change them and switch on the positivity. The more often you practise this technique (down the street, in the pub, walking into your place of work) the easier it is to do when you really need it... *like when you are speaking in public.* You can also use it in everyday life situations and for bluffing in poker... it works!

Let's try something else.

Find a space that is private and allows you to move around. Your task is to adopt a specific role (proper acting fun now) and use this character to determine how you walk and feel inside.

Your first role is as follows. You are the head teacher of a very posh private school, which only admits the richest and most privileged children in the world. Now walk around as if this is you. Notice everything again. Your body, your energy, your emotions. How does this feel to you? And how is your body reacting?

Now you are the head teacher of the worst state school in the UK, where most of the children (and their parents) are very badly behaved. You feel fear quite a lot in this role, and often wonder where the next fight or stumbling block is going to come from. Now how are you walking? What are your emotions like? What do you feel in your stomach?

Now you are a homeless person. You have no home and no money and you live on the streets. What pace are you walking at? How do you feel? What emotions are coming up?

Now you are a confident public speaker, knowledgeable about your topic and ready to deliver a great talk. Your shoulders are back and you are feeling on top of the world. Really lavish this role. It's one of the best ones to be in!

Now think back...

Which roles were easier? Which roles made you feel positive

and confident? Which roles made you feel negative? Were there any similarities between roles?

You may have discovered that some of the roles felt positive and some felt negative. The real question here is why? Why did one scenario make you feel good and another not so good? Similar situations may have invoked a different response. Why?

The reason for this is down to the same phenomenon that occurs when two people in an identical situation interpret very different experiences.

Your Perception.

Perception is very important in public speaking as it is the foundation of how you prepare, how your emotions are formed and how the event will go.

Let's look at more research here to help your understanding of how perception plays a key role in why you are succeeding or failing in public speaking. It can also apply to other areas of your life too.

In 1928, two American sociologists (William and Dorothy Thomas) formulated The Thomas Theorem. They summed this theory up by one simple but very important quote:

"If men define situations as real, they are real in their consequences."

In other words, if you believe something to be true, then be-cause of your actions that follow, it will be. Your perception of a situation will determine how you react and consequently that will affect the outcome. Even if I say to you: "You are a brilliant public speaker", if you strongly don't believe me then you will react according to your perception and not what I tell you.

Evidently, the Thomas Theorem makes a lot of practical sense. Having a positive or negative belief declared as truth in your own mind (even when it is actually false) is likely to sufficiently influence you so that your own reactions ultimately fulfil this idea of yourself.

You've probably heard of the "Self-fulfilling Prophecy" in which a prediction is formed that in turn influences the outcomes to thereby prove the prediction to be true.

Do you see how your perception of yourself in public speaking can be key to how well you perform?

There is much research out there which looks at teacher expectation and student attainment. For example, Jussim, Smith, Madon & Palumbo (1998) and Alvidrez & Weinstein, (1999) found significant correlations between the two. The higher the teacher's expectations were for a particular pupil, the higher the pupil's academic achievement. Furthermore, there are strong indications that student grades may be biased by the teacher's own expectations and perceptions of each student. A worrying thought, isn't it, that a teacher is likely to grade an assignment based on their belief about the student's ability rather than the work the student has actually submitted?

Yet, it's obvious really. The more you believe something to be true about someone or something, the more true it becomes in your head, in *your reality* and if you are in a position of power or influence, like a teacher or leader, you could force this reality to extend to those around you too.

Let's look at one of the most well-known Shakespearean plays, Macbeth. It's arguably a great example of a self-fulfilling prophecy. If you haven't read or seen Macbeth performed, you'll still get the general idea. Near the beginning of the play, three witches tell Macbeth that he will eventually become king. Later they warn him about his best friend whose son will eventually rule in his stead. Driven by this prophecy (and scheming) Macbeth kills the king and his best friend in order to keep himself and his bloodline safe. Yet, this fuels his former best friend's son to seek revenge and consequently Macbeth is killed by him. Do you see the Self-fulfilling Prophecy here? If the witches had not told Macbeth to watch out for his friend, then he may not have killed him and thus not spurred on his own death by his friend's vengeful son. This play is a rather dramatic way to interpret the power of perception and the self-fulfilling prophecy.

In reality, the Thomas Theorem, the Self-fulfilling Prophesy Theory and Theories of Expectations in education are very similar to The Law of Attraction which became very popular in the 90s and is still going strong, with interesting books on "Cosmic Ordering" by Barbel Mohr and others. A mainstream book you may have heard of is "The Secret" by Rhonda Byrne. All of these books focus on the simple notion that *like attracts like*. By expecting all good things (and asking for them) you can bring about positive results and manifest the life you want.

According to the Law of Attraction, your thoughts and words form your intentions and consequently your actions. What you give out, you get back. What you believe to be coming, will arrive. This is similar to the self-fulling prophecy but with the possibility of a much better and more positive outcome, as long as positivity and great expectations are in place.

Perception and expectation play a crucial role in the way we live life. Coming back to public speaking specifically, it is very important then to check in with your *perception* before you even start your preparation. Make sure it's coming from a good place, so you can set yourself up for a positive outcome.

If your natural response is: "I'm terrible at this" or "I'm not that good" or "I'll probably mess up", then you are setting yourself up for failure. On the basis of all my years of training public speakers, coupled with over a hundred years of experts' psychological research and the simple law of attraction knowledge, everything indicates that perception and expectations affect the way you perform in life.

And if you are still not convinced about the power of perception, think about the Placebo Effect in medical science. A placebo is a form of treatment given to patients that does not actually do anything to the physical body. It's used as a psychological way to treat the patient, so they believe they are getting medicine, when in actual fact they are getting a sugar pill or an injection of saline, etc. Because the patient *expects* to get better and indeed *perceives* a full recovery, very often there is a measurable beneficial effect such as pain reduction or improved blood pressure. There can also be negative effects such as headaches, feelings of sickness and a lot worse. **It all depends on what the patient *expects* the drug to do to them.**

Bearing in mind the overwhelming evidence here, I ask you one question:

How can you change your perceptions, thoughts and words to make sure you give yourself the best possible chance of succeeding? What can you say, do or think to help with years of negative brain patterning?

A simple answer to help you is:

Expect to succeed.

Tune in to your own perception and be honest with yourself. If your perception is negative then change it, just like you did in the previous exercise when you changed your emotions! Then see what happens.

For public speaking, I find the best affirmation is:

"I'm a confident public speaker, knowledgeable about my topic and ready to do this!"

However, if that doesn't ring true yet, or you feel a bit of resistance, take it down a notch.

Try some of these:

"I'm looking forward to my next event"

"I admire how far I've come!"

"I'm a confident public speaker!"

"I expect things to go well"

If you suffer from anxiety at times, try these simple affirmations every day:

"I expect all good things from today onwards"

"I'm learning to be a good public speaker."

"I feel in control and balanced today."

"I feel relaxed and calm today."

You can also extend this to your area of work in general (as negative perceptions tend to have a long root).

Instead of: "I hate this report!" try *"I'm going to be open minded and do the best I can."*

Or instead of: "I don't know anything about this!" try *"I'm going to learn as much as I can in the time I have."*

Once you change your perception into something positive, check in with your emotions. Make sure they are also positive and serving you. Your goal is to do well and all these changes to your patterns of thought are going to help you.

To conclude this section, let's think about the common public speaking issues again, such as shaking, voice trembling and messing up. As you have read, feedback from coaches or the general public which tell you, "not to do this" or only highlight your issues by saying, "are you aware you are going red?" are not helpful. The problem is not the issues themselves but the way your body is reacting to something internal, which 9 times out of 10 is a result of your own perception. These issues are the outward display of the expectations and the limitations you place on your body and mind by having these beliefs. Being aware of your perceptions and emotions enables you to alter these states by the methods we have just learned and by using some of the tools covered in the next few chapters.

The most important thing to remember is to ***expect to improve.***

Perceive yourself in a positive light.

TOP TIP

Always look inward and be aware of how you feel. Leave any negativity at the door, behind you! Be professional. This is your job. This is your role. Step up and go for it!

Cairns

Chapter Six

Super Objective

I now want to introduce a great acting method, which I encourage my speakers to use when preparing their talks, speeches, presentations and interviews. It is something I train all my acting students in.

It is called "The Super Objective". The Super Objective was originally a concept developed by Konstantin Stanislavski, a Russian theatre practitioner and actor of the 1900s. Stanislavski is a founding father in the acting world. He introduced and pushed for- ward the world of characterisation, naturalism and realism. You may have heard the concept of "method acting"? This was built on the foundations of Stanislavski's principles.

One of the most important factors to consider when using Stan-islavski's method is the Objective and Action of the character. In laymen's terms it means understanding what your character is trying to achieve. What do they want? What is their objective? And what do they do in order to achieve this objective? What is their action?

For actors, any given scene may hold 2 or 3 different objectives a character is trying to achieve. But there is also an over-arching objective threading every scene together and which the character is aiming to achieve throughout the entire play or film. It is known as the "Super Objective". This is what your character *really* wants. It doesn't change from scene to scene unless a major character transformation occurs (often just at the end of the play). It is always at the root of everything a character does.

For example, imagine you are playing a middle-aged male character who hates his job. This man's Super Objective might be: ***I want to be valued.*** Since he doesn't ever achieve this in his current job, each day his objective might be: ***I want a new job.*** So his daily action becomes: I search job listings online.

How does this apply to public speaking?

Let's start by looking at why you are reading this book.

Perhaps your personal or professional Super Objective in the context of public speaking is: *"I want to improve my public speaking"*. So your action would be: "I read this book".

Any objective should always start with "I want" and only be a few words. This is so you can keep coming back to the objective without getting confused.

Before you start your research and planning for any public speaking event, ask yourself: What is my Super Objective? What am I *really* trying to achieve?

You may have a few ideas spinning in your head, and that's okay, but try to settle on the most important one which will inform the best action.

Here are some great examples:

"I want to impress my boss"

"I want to share my story"

"I want to sell my product"

"I want to do the best I can"

"I want to speak confidently"

Your super objective forms the very structure of your presentation. With your Super Objective in mind, you will create your talk, speech or answers based around what it is you want to achieve. Therefore, you must know what you want before you start. Don't try and find it later. Have a direction before you begin, a pre-determined goal.

And stick to it.

It may be comforting to know, I've never worked with anyone who has chosen the "wrong" objective. Some objectives can be stronger than others and some can work better for you. That's why you should take a moment to decide what you *actually* want. Then tailor it back to how you achieve this from your presentation.

For example, let's say you have to deliver a report at your next team meeting. Your Super Objective might be: *"I want to get a promotion"*. While this is an obvious and strong Super Objective, you need to break it down a little. Perhaps to get a promotion, you first need to be noticed by your superiors in the best possible light. Therefore at the next team meeting, your objective could be: *"I want to deliver this report with confidence"*. It's not your Super Objective but it is a positive objective that you can achieve and it may very well move you a step closer to your super objective of gaining that promotion later on.

Having a strong Super Objective and day to day objectives helps to form an **intention**. Make sure you *expect* the outcomes to be positive. Have a good perception of yourself and the event. The above objective, "I want to deliver the report with confidence", will help you from the beginning as you start to plan and organise your contribution to the team meeting around wanting to achieve that objective.

Take it step by step, scene by scene, talk by talk. And remember your over-arching Super Objective, in the case of the above: "I want a promotion."

TOP TIP

Keep objectives simple and to the point. Most of all, make them meaningful and individual to you. Give each objective truth and positivity to offer yourself the best chance of achieving it. And make sure it's only about you and no-one else. For example: "I want to be better than so and so", isn't a strong objective. "I want to deliver a fantastic, engaging report", is strong, as it only involves you being the best you can be!

Chapter Seven

Stress

Speaking in public can create a lot of stress in the mind and body. One of the most important parts of my job is coaching individuals on how to cope with this type of stress. Learning how to relax and control those nerves (which can trigger social anxiety) is fundamental to becoming a confident public speaker.

Right now, if you are the sort of presenter who gets very nervous, you are more likely to speak too quickly, get tongue-tied or have too many thoughts at once, which can lead to a panic state. If you suffer from anxiety, you are very likely to get nauseous or even hyperventilate. Perhaps you avoid public speaking at all costs.

If you suffer from any of these nervous symptoms, it can be very stressful. If you've tried to get help and have been met with the usual comments of: "slow down", "don't shake" or "chill out", then I really feel for you. These comments are so unhelpful, especially when you feel like that.

For those of you struggling, what we really need to do is work on lowering your heart-rate, slowing down your thoughts and getting you into a relaxed frame of mind. The most effective way to do this is simply by controlling your breathing.

Controlled breathing will send the right amount of oxygen to your body which in turn, will bring that high nervous energy back down into what I call the *Safe Zone*. You will feel comfortable and more in control. And consequently, you will have conquered most of the common public speaking issues (like speaking too fast and shaking etc.) as you will have automatically *slowed down* and grounded yourself.

Breath work is the foundation of all relaxation methods and vocal technique training. Before we start to learn more about this, let's see where you are at to begin with!

Take a deep breath in.

Be aware of your shoulders, belly and chest.

What moved most? Did your shoulders go up? Did your chest rise? Did your stomach push outward?

Breathe out if you have not already.

The best way to breathe is straight into your belly, so your stomach rises as you breathe in and deflates as your breathe out. Your shoulders should not move at all and your chest, only slightly. If you find your shoulders and chest move a lot, try this exercise lying down, on your back.

Animals and babies are the best at this. They instinctively know the best way to breathe. But as life gets busy and we strive for the quickest and easiest way to achieve what we want or need, we start to breathe into our chest. Consequently, our shoulders become the place of burden, tension and stress. Breathing that way also restricts how effective we can be with our voice. To use our voice to its full potential, our bodies need to be relaxed, so breath can flow.

So... let's get you breathing properly!

It's best to do this exercise lying down, perhaps on your bed. It takes about 5 minutes.

Be aware of how you feel...

How *do* you feel right now?

Place one hand on your chest and one on your lower stomach. As you breathe in, try to fill up the bottom part of your stomach. The hand on your stomach should rise up as you breathe in and then fall as you breathe out. Be sure to release all your air on the out breath. Keep your shoulders and chest relaxed. Most of the work should be in your stomach. Lying down makes relaxing your shoulders and chest a lot easier as your weight is supported by the floor or bed. This is why it is good to practise lying down, until you are breathing into your stomach naturally again.

Breathe in for a count of 4. *Hold for a count of 2.*

Breathe out for a count for 4. *Hold for a count of 2.*

Breathe in for a count of 4. *Hold for a count of 2.*

Breathe out for a count for 6. *Hold for a count of 2.*

Breathe in for a count of 4. *Hold for a count of 2.*

Breathe out for a count for 8. *Hold for a count of 2.*

Do this again, each time increasing your exhale by 2 seconds (always holding for a count of 2 after you have exhaled all your breath) until you struggle to complete the out-breath.

After you have finished this routine, how do you feel?

I'm going to take a shot in the dark here and guess that you feel a *little* more relaxed. This exercise has only taken a couple of minutes. Can you imagine what would happen if you did this for 5 minutes before or after a stressful event?

Controlled breathing is one of the first steps to meditation. It allows you to get back to your centre and back to the present moment. It stills your mind whilst delivering fresh, clean air to your body, which as a Speaker, is highly beneficial.

You may have also noticed that the out-breath was harder as you went up in exhalation durations. Try this exercise again, and this time hold some air back when you start your exhalation so you can last the whole way when you breathe out. This means you are not just working on relaxing your body and mind, but you are also starting to train in breath control which is essential to your vocal training and the ability to reduce those nerves at the drop of a hat, or in this case, at the drop of your diaphragm (the muscle primarily used in breath work).

Keep practising this exercise. You can change the numbers around too. For example try this:

Breathe in for a count of 6. *Hold for a count of 4.*

Breathe out for a count for 10. *Hold for a count of 2.*

Breathe in for a count of 4. *Hold for a count of 6.*

Breathe out for a count for 8. *Hold for a count of 4.*

Breathe in for a count of 2. *Hold for a count of 2.*

Breathe out for a count for 12. *Hold for a count of 2.*

Breathe in for a count of 6. *Hold for a count of 4.*

Breathe out for a count for 14. *Hold for a count of 4.*

Breathe in for a count of 6. *Hold for a count of 8.*

Breathe out for a count for 10. *Hold for a count of 2.*

Long exhalations really help build breath control. Make sure you mix it up to keep working on your breath and ultimately relaxing your mind and body.

Breathing also acts as the foundation for your voice work. Being able to have a strong, reliable voice starts with breath control. As Speakers, this is another key area you will want to develop.

Training in breath work and vocal technique is covered extensively in my online course. You'll explore many more types of breath work and vocal exercises with clear examples and easy to follow guided practices, including tips for *which* breath to use at different types of events and situations. You'll also have a whole module dedicated to meditation and *a guided meditation track that will help on the day of your presentation and the night before!*

TOP TIP

If you find yourself thrusted into a stressful situation, and
haven't had time to plan, warm up or relax beforehand,
then here is a good tip. Stand up, take a breath in and raise
your shoulders up to your ears as you do so. Pause and
then release your breath and let your shoulders sink back
down. This is where your shoulders should be and already
you will have re- leased some tension. Do this three times
before your presentation or stressful event.

Chapter Eight

Uniform

It's a well-known fact that the way we dress can influence other people's perceptions of us. We take a lot of social cues and make swift judgements based on how a person is dressed. For example, imagine you are holding a job interview for a new opening in a law firm. Your first interviewee turns up in jogging bottoms, a creased dirty t-shirt and old tennis shoes. What would be your initial thoughts about this person? Would they make a good first impression on you? Unless that person had a very impressive resumé and an interesting explanation for their chosen attire like: "I saved the world today", they are probably not going to get the job. If they can't be bothered making an effort for the interview, then they probably can't be bothered working hard for you either, right? Equally, a man dressed in a pristine Armani suit wearing smart, polished shoes who is sitting on the pavement with a "homeless" sign isn't going to convince you to give him money.

In a working environment, we dress the part to influence people's perception of us and the "third party perspective".

However, as the Pressure System is about looking within, let's consider the effect your clothes and attire can have on you. And consequently, your own perception of yourself, your role and your energy.

In psychology, a fairly recent study by Hajo Adam and Adam Galinsky (2012) introduces a new term called "Enclothed Cognition" to explain the precise influence clothes have on our psycho- logical processes. They proved what you wear can significantly al- ter your thoughts and consequently your actions!

Adam and Galinsky conducted experiments in which individuals performed attention-related tasks, such as being shown two similar pictures on a screen and spotting any differences as quickly as possible. This included, for example, when the word red is writ- ten in the colour green. They found that when the individuals were wearing lab coats, their attention increased. What is even more interesting for us as public speakers, is that when the lab coats were referred to as "doctors coats", this increased attention even more, demonstrating two independent factors when considering Enclothed Cognition:

1) The symbolic meaning of the clothes to an individual

2) The physical experience of wearing them.

The first factor represents what the clothes mean to the wearer. For example, does an expensive suit mean power, confidence and success? Does wearing glasses make you feel more intelligent?

Let's look at your clothes right now.

What do they symbolise to you? Work? Summer? Winter?

Fun? Creative? Professional?

The second factor is what these clothes make you feel like when you wear them. For example, do your clothes make you feel important? Confident? Lazy?

Dressing the part isn't just about third party perceptive, it's about how you perceive your clothes to be and how they fit into your psyche. As an individual, you've got to wear what makes *you* feel good, as well as what society would expect in your given environment.

In other words, if you are a woman who feels more powerful in a trouser suit (but scared you'll look masculine or be perceived un-favourably) experiment with different types that have a more feminine flare. Don't just go for a dress or skirt if it doesn't feel right. Do what works for you and fits with the occasion so that you feel powerful, comfortable and confident.

For public speaking, consider the context. What would an open, confident and knowledgeable speaker look like to you? Or consider what a successful applicant might look like for a particular job interview.

If you are a free spirt, and really do feel more "professional" in jeans and a t-shirt, then find a balance that works for those outsiders who may make snap judgements solely based on your appearance. Such as smart jeans, with a smart tucked in shirt and smart shoes.

Remember: Most people do feel more professional, powerful, important and successful in an expensive suit or uniform for what-ever industry they are in.

Let's practise something.

You can do this anywhere as long as you have a quiet minute where you don't have to communicate with anyone. Grab a pen and paper too. You may wish to do this exercise a few times with different scenarios as it's very useful!

Think of an event you are speaking at soon. Or an interview you have coming up. Or think about your work or your personal life. Any situation where you would like to feel better about yourself or be more successful.

Now think about what a successful person in this situation would wear. Sketch it out or write descriptions.

Now imagine yourself wearing this. Really see it in your mind. How does it fit your body? How does it look on you?

Next step, go online or head out to the shops and see if this type of outfit exists (I'm sure it does). Try on the clothes if you can and be aware of how they make you feel. You might surprise yourself!

If you feel "false" or are thinking, "that won't look good on me", then carry on to the next chapter and come back to this exercise later.

TOP TIP

Telephone interview coming up? Dress the part! What you are wearing will affect your body, voice, actions, reactions, cognition, brain functions and thus your ability to answer all those questions well. Make an effort and see what happens!

Chapter Nine

Role-Play

As I'm sure you will now realise, the skills of an actor and performer are very useful for public speakers. You rarely get an actor who finds it difficult to speak in public. Yes, some actors may feel nervous but their training kicks in and they get on with it. Actors either have a natural talent for being on stage and film or they learn their craft. Either way, all performers benefit from skill development and training their mind, body and voice.

And that's what public speaking is. A performance. It's all about stepping into the role of something or someone for a short time to get the job done.

We have many roles in life. The role of the father or mother. The role of the daughter or son. The role of the professional manager versus the role of the chilled-out husband as he lounges on the sofa watching TV on his day off. We all have roles and costumes we step into throughout the day and throughout our life.

Even new speakers who come to me and say, "I just want to be myself up there". That is great but what part of themselves is it better to be?

People spend their whole lives wondering who they are and what their purpose is. Motivational speakers, philosophers and spiritual leaders makes millions from helping people to *find them-selves* or *their purpose in life.*

Actors see many different purposes and many different roles. And that's what makes them happy. The idea of role-play is very important in public speaking. It's something all actors know! And we apply this each time we have to speak in public or perform. New speakers can often misunderstand the concept of role-play and acting, discounting their value, perhaps believing it to mean they are being false or telling lies.

I'm finding more and more people don't want to *fake it until they make it.* They want to be sincere and genuine.

And while this is very possible if you are presenting, you must remember you are still on stage, and you are still performing. Being able to step into a role will help you deliver a stronger presentation and also ensure you retain your integrity, reduce your vulnerability, and make it easier to step back into another role after your event. For example, returning to your family at night after a huge, successful day, without losing perspective on the most important things in your life (i.e. those you love).

When you are presenting, going for an interview, or giving a speech at a wedding, it's always going to be you. You just want a specific part of you to step into. The part that's going to sell your product or get you that job offer. Not the part that lazes around on a Sunday afternoon.

I understand people want to be sincere. I do too. So I don't ask clients to "*fake it until you make it.*" I say: "Imagine until you be-come."

Like an actor, you need to know your character, know your role, use your imagination, step into that role and become that role! Perform it. Do your job. Then drop your role and come back to your real life. To those you love, or places you feel strong and at home in. Knowing when to drop the role and relax is just as important as getting into it. As most actors know, they can't sustain their character for long periods, as it's not healthy. If you are choosing to play the *Successful Motivational Speaker,* that's going to take up a lot of your energy. So know when to call upon your role and know when to let it rest.

If you are reading this and still have doubt in your ability to perform, or successfully carry out a role, just *imagine* you are a confident public speaker. Perceive and expect this. Then one day you will be presenting and you will realise you no longer need to imagine. Perhaps you'll no longer question why you are there or wonder if anyone knows you don't "belong" (the impostor syndrome). In fact, very often speakers like you *become* many years before they even realise it.

How do we step into roles?

Even if you are not an actor, you can do this. Let's look back to Chapter Five: Emotions, when you were given an occupation or stereotypical character. You were playing around and seeing how situations and characters felt, based on your own perceptions. Perhaps some helped you feel confident, while others made you uncomfortable. As speakers, we must select the correct role that we wish to step into, to best achieve our objective.

Grab a pen and paper and let's go through a few steps.

This exercise can be done almost anywhere (as long as you don't have to communicate with anyone). It will take up to 5 minutes.

Think of an event, presentation, meeting or situation you have coming up that relates to public speaking.

What is your **objective**?

An example for a presentation might be: "I want to sell my product" or for a team meeting: "I want to deliver my report with clarity and authority".

What is your **perception** of this event right now?

If it's negative, then change it into something positive. Examples might be: "I expect it to go well" or "I expect to deliver my presentation with confidence and clarity" or "I will speak with confidence and engage my team".

What are your **emotions** regarding this event?

If there is any- thing negative, be aware and then try to change them into positive emotions like you did in Chapter 5. Examples may be: "I feel confident, calm and prepared" or "I feel excited at the challenge".

Now think about what **role** would best serve you to help achieve your objective.

For example: "A confident public speaker, knowledgeable about my topic and ready to do this" or "A successful entrepreneur and motivational speaker" or "A knowledgeable, passionate and confident team player and leader who is open and assertive".

After you've considered the best role, then think about what **uniform** you would wear to suit this role? Examples may be smart Jeans, smart belt, smart shirt, shiny shoes, slick hair and a trim beard. Or normal work clothes, hair tied back, red lipstick, red nails and a cute black leather case.

The procedure you have just carried out is invaluable when you start preparing for your speaking event. You will automatically design your talk around achieving your objective.

With practice, the way you approach your presentation may start to deviate from this basic structure and that is fine. Experimenting means we can learn what works and what doesn't for us, as individual speakers. **Make sure you do the above exercise before you start any preparation**, to you give yourself the best possible start.

Crossing the Line

Now let's try stepping into the role using a practice exercise I call, *The Line Technique.*

You'll need a bit of space and you'll want to be alone for about 5 minutes.

Stand up and look down at your feet.

Imagine there is a line in front of you. Where you are now represents the present moment. Over the line represents where you want to be, who you want to be, what role you wish to step into, and how you want to feel.

Be aware of what the line looks like to you? What colour is it? What width? What depth? Does it have height? Or is dug into the ground?

Recall the role you want to step into. Or use my go-to affirmation: "I'm a confident public speaker, knowledgeable about my topic and ready to do this!"

Be aware of where you are right now, and where you want to be....

And now CROSS THE LINE! STEP UP to this new role!

Walk around and see how you feel.

This is a great exercise to help you get into your role. You can use The Line Technique throughout the day. In fact, the more you practise crossing the line and stepping up into your role, the easier it will become.

You can do it in public too and no-one will know. For example, if you are at work and feel a bit down, pull your shoulders back, imagine you are feeling confident, open and happy, *cross the line* and see what happens!

Another question I get asked from my clients is: "*how can I step into the role I need, when I am caught off guard*".

For example, perhaps you are out at the shops with your kids and you randomly spot the director of your dream company (the one you are dying to work for), or someone who could really help your business thrive.

How do you speak to them, without sounding too pushy or annoying?

How can you step up and become that "role" when you aren't prepared?

It's not possible for me to cover absolutely everything in this short book (as it's designed to be quick and easy), so instead, I've created another secret bonus just for my readers!

Everything you need to know about the best way to present, promote and sell yourself in the shortest period of time is in my special training bonus: *How to Seize the Moment, Step Up & Be Remembered.*

I created this, so you can make the most of opportunities that come your way and never be caught off guard again!

You can get it here for free:

https://www.professionalperformanceassocia-tion.com/Book_Bonus_Training

TOP TIP

You can also use the Line Technique when you've had a bad day and don't want to carry it home with you. Use the front door as your line and once you've crossed it you are going to leave all the stressful energy you picked up behind you, step- ping into a more relaxed version of yourself.

Clare Cairns

Chapter Ten

Energy

--·————— °♦° ———·--

Energy exists. Actors work with it every single day. It's our stage presence. For speakers it's your star quality. The life force and power behind how you deliver your speech that will make people turn their heads, notice and engage with you.

As performers and speakers, we must learn to control our energy so that we can call upon it when we need it and become better at what we do.

Let's practise tapping into it right now.

You can do this anywhere; it takes about 5 minutes.

Stand up with your feet hip distance apart or wider.

Shake your whole body. Swing your arms, bend your knees, shake your feet and hands. Give your whole body a big shake out for at least a minute.

Rub the palms of your hands together vigorously for 1-2 minutes.

Now part your hands about 10 cm apart. Be aware of any

tingling or other sensations you may experience.

Pull your hands wider apart, then bring them close together but not touching.

Widen and shorten the space between your palms in a pulsing movement.

Do you feel anything? Tingles? Changes in temperature? A magnetic pull in the space between your palms?

This is a simple example of how to feel your energy! If you don't feel anything, you need more practice. It might take a few days to build on this.

I always recommend practising several times a day until you start feeling more activity in the space between your palms. This is you raising your energy and gaining more control over it.

Good awareness and control over your energy is an important skill to master. We can use different forms of energy to succeed in different situations. For example, speaking to one person requires a very different energy than when speaking to 100 people. It's not necessarily about adjusting the volume of your voice (as you would probably have a mic if you are delivering a talk to 100 people). It's about adjusting your energetic projection. Making things bigger internally, so you can project it externally and reach more people. Think of an actor on stage compared to an actor in a film. A theatre actor often uses more energy and bigger movements than a film actor, who normally strives for fewer gestures and more "eye" acting. As a speaker, you are very likely to be involved much more in a theatre type set up, in front of a large, live audience with whom you need to interact; therefore, you need more energy.

However, if you have too much energy you could become *hyperactive,* which can be a disaster for speakers. Examples of this include speaking too quickly, over-thinking and being unable to formulate your ideas into effective sentences. A speaker with too much energy can appear manic and nervous, making their audience feel uncomfortable. To control this, you need to practise your breath work and slow things down. Meditation in the run up to your event will really help.

Likewise, if you don't have enough energy, your presentation could be *boring*. Perhaps your voice becomes a monotone or you include very little interaction or engagement with the audience. There are things you can do to gain more energy without stimulants like coffee or sugar, which are actually counterproductive to your speaking. Coupled with nerves, these stimulants can send you into overdrive and hyperactivity.

High Energy Practices

Since we all have moments of tiredness though, here are some great *High Energy* practices.

You'll need somewhere with a bit of space and privacy. This will last about 5 minutes.

Spend 20 seconds doing the following exercises and notice how you feel emotionally and physically.

First of all, clap your hands and smile.

Now jump up and down on the spot.

Now raise your arms above your head on an in-breath and lower them down on the out-breath.

Finally, stand with your feet hip distant apart with a straight spine and neck. Imagine the soles of your feet are roots, that go through the floor, through the ground, right into the fiery core of the earth. Now take some of that fire back up, through the soles of your feet, right into your belly.

Did any of these make you feel more energised?

Which actions did you like? Which ones could you use in future to give yourself more energy?

All these are great exercises that actors use to warm up or just to give them an energetic boost before they go on stage.

You may have heard of Power Poses, made famous by Amy Cudder, the American social psychologist in her 2012 TED talk on Body Language. She states that adopting certain poses can cause positive or negative hormonal and behavioural changes. For example, taking on a "superhero" pose makes people feel more empowered.

Around 2014, I had lots of clients come and ask me about this 'new thing'. Yet the concept has been around for a very long time. In the performing arts, we often move the shape of our bodies to shift our energy, change our emotions and flow through scenes. Michael Chekhov, a great pioneer in the acting world, came up with the idea of the Psychological Gesture in the 1900s. This is where the actor uses a series of collective movements or just one solid body position (like a live sculpture) to sum up the thoughts and feelings inside the character, including their desires and objectives. This helps connect the actor to the character.

For example, a character who is feeling depressed, lost and scared may have a psychological gesture of a person sitting on the floor, with their knees drawn into their chest and their head hanging down. A character who is full of confidence and positivity might have a psychological gesture of a person with a tall, proud stance, with their back upright, their chest sticking out, arms open and their head held high. When the actor has to play either character, he will adopt their psychological gesture and connect with them immediately.

I use a similar technique with public speakers, which I call Energy Poses.

In public speaking, what we want is not just to change our body language but to *tap into the right energy* so our body, mind and voice manifest the most appropriate form for us. It does it naturally!

Remember the power of role-play and selecting the right role to achieve our objective? After we know what role to step into, we can then form an Energy Pose to sum up the psychology behind this role. For example, if we adopt an Energy Pose that sums up 'Positive, confident, assured, prepared and happy', we can reap the benefits. Adopting the psychology of the body position (and what it means to us as an individual) gives us so much more identity than just standing like a superhero in the superhero power pose. This is because we have created a pose, we have taken charge and we know what it means to connect with this Energy Pose.

One of my go-to Energy Poses for public speakers is as follows.

Stand in a neutral position, feet hip-distance apart, straight spine and neck. Relax your knees so they are slightly bent. Reach up to the sky with your arms. Feel the energy from the Earth in the soles of your feet and also the energy from the sky in the tips of your fingers. Feel your own energy inside your body, and in one big movement push your arms out to the side, so you are in a T-shape. Imagine your energy stretching beyond your hands so it touches the wall, then goes through the wall and beyond the room you are in.

Spend the next few minutes experimenting. Think of a role you wish to step into. Then try to come up with your own Energy Pose.

What position makes you feel good in the role? Feel free to put on some uplifting music or use anything that empowers you to look inward and then express it outward!

Be aware of how you feel.

Do you feel stronger? More confident? More Powerful? Is this something you can use to make you feel like a *confident Public Speaker, knowledgeable about your topic and ready to engage?*

If so, you can use this as your energy pose! If not, keep working on it. You could also look at yoga poses to help you, such as Warrior 1, 2 or 3.

Remember: energy exists. Actors and performers use it every day. Some people have that "je ne sais quoi" naturally. You can *feel* them as they enter a room. You can learn to do this by practising to build and raise your energy through the above exercises.

You can also apply the Energy Pose you just learned or created when you prepare for your presentation. This will ensure your mind and body are ready to adopt the correct energy to help you achieve your objective. Practise your chosen pose before you rehearse your talk to form a trigger for your energy activation. When you warm up in the morning of your presentation, give your energy pose more effort than usual so it lasts the whole day. If you get a toilet break or a chance to re-do it before your talk, take it! And as you walk up to your performing space, use the Line Technique, cross the line, pull your shoulders back, and make a commitment to do the best you can.

TOP TIP

Mark your presentation slides or notes with a star shape or asterisk to remind you to build your energy. Do it every 2-3 slides, so that you mindfully keep your energy going through- out your talk.

Clare Cairns

Chapter Eleven
Congratulations!

You've just read and practised some of the most fundamental tools, tips and tricks to become a more confident, captivating and successful speaker. *Well done!*

If you need more help (for example maybe you have an event coming up and you need to stand out) then make sure you check out "Public Speaking Without Fear" my online program.

It's full of videos, downloadable cheat-sheets, action-sheets, checklists, templates, audios and much more.

You'll also get bundle packed bonuses such as How to Present to Camera as well as become part of the inner circle of The PPA Club.

Check it out here:

www.professionalperformanceassociation.com

Remember to use the code READBOOK at checkout to get a big discount off the program price!

And don't forget to pick up your FREE exclusive training bonuses here:

https://www.professionalperformanceassociation.com/Book_B onus_Training

Now before we finish, let us go through a quick re-cap of some of the most important points in each section of this book, to keep reinforcing those skills in the meantime.

Remember to use the PRESSURE system to help guide you.

We will do that now.

Prepare

Know your Topic

Bin the Script

Rehearse

Practise with your new knowledge and skills

Find your own unique way of speaking

Build many neurological connections around your topic by simply rehearsing

Emotions

Be aware

Check-in with your perceptions and expectations towards the event

Change any negative emotions into positive ones

Super objective

Know your Objective

Know what you want

Stress

Relax

Breathe

Visualise Success

Uniform

Wear the right clothes for you and your audience

Role-Play

Find the most suitable role that you can 'play' to achieve your objective

"Imagine until you become"

Cross the line with the Line Technique

Step up to the Challenge

Energy

Find your Energy

Build and Raise with Energy Poses

Keep your energy up!

If you have a presentation, interview or event coming up, you can now apply all that you have learned...

Do your **P**reparation

Rehearse, practising your delivery

Check-in with your **E**motions to make sure all is positive

Use breathing relaxation tools to calm your **S**tress

Select your **S**uper objective

Choose your **U**niform

Decide the best **R**ole that fits your objective

Raise your **E**nergy and nail your talk!

You can re-visit these chapters at any time.

Before the Curtain Closes...

I hope you realise now that public speaking does not have to be an ordeal. It can be highly enjoyable and very rewarding.

Just apply the tips and tricks of *the acting world* and remember the PRESSURE system to guide you.

And say "YES" to public speaking. Take part in opportunities that allow you to grow, practise and learn.

Above all, **believe in yourself and expect the best.**

You CAN be a confident, public speaker. You CAN create and deliver a truly memorable, first class speech and presentation. Empower yourself and you WILL be successful at your next event.

I would like to finish by saying a huge thank you to all my family, friends, clients, actors and fellow expert coaches and directors. Especially to my father, brother and amazing husband for their endless support, guidance and love towards me and my writing. To everyone who has played a part in getting this book out there, not forgetting Ethos Writing and Class Moustache Publishing, thank you!

"I hope my book helps to improve the lives of all public speakers, especially those with anxiety or nerves and encourages everyone to enjoy communicating, speaking and sharing their stories (now that they have some valuable acting training behind them)!"

Printed in Great Britain
by Amazon